BRAIN ACADEMY
SUPERMATHS

Louise Moore, Pete Crawford
and Richard Cooper

Mission File 4
Years 5-6

Produced in association with

nace
National Association
for Able Children
in Education

RISING STARS

Rising Stars are grateful to the following people for their support in developing this series: Sue Mordecai, Julie Fitzpatrick, Johanna Raffan, Belle Wallace and Clive Tunnicliffe.

nace

NACE, PO Box 242, Arnolds Way, Oxford OX2 9FR
www.nace.co.uk

Rising Stars UK Ltd, 22 Grafton Street, London W1S 4EX
www.risingstars-uk.com

Every effort has been made to trace copyright holders and obtain their permission for the use of copyright materials. The authors and publisher will gladly receive information enabling them to rectify any error or omission in subsequent editions.

All facts are correct at time of going to press.

Published 2007
Text, design and layout © Rising Stars UK Ltd.

Editorial Consultant: Jean Carnall
Cover design: Burville-Riley
Design: Pentacor**big**
Illustrations: Cover – Burville-Riley / Characters – Bill Greenhead

All rights reserved. No part of this publication may be reproduced, stored in a retrieval system, or transmitted, in any form by any means, electronic, mechanical, photocopying, recording or otherwise, without the prior permission of Rising Stars.

British Library Cataloguing in Publication Data.
A CIP record for this book is available from the British Library.

ISBN: 978-1-84680-233-1

Printed by Craft Print International Ltd, Singapore

CONTENTS

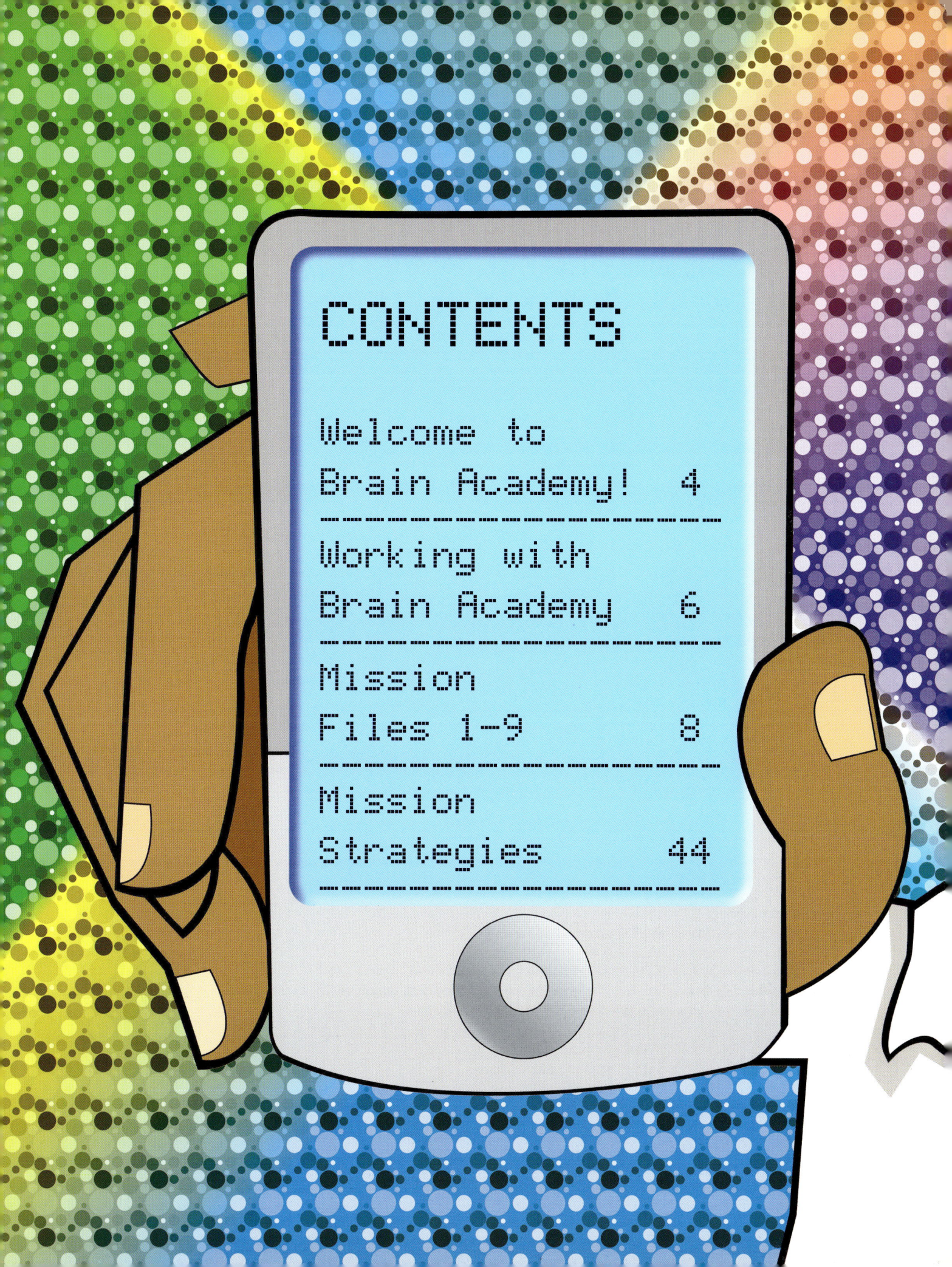

Welcome to Brain Academy!   4

Working with Brain Academy   6

Mission Files 1-9   8

Mission Strategies   44

Welcome to Brain Academy!

Welcome to Brain Academy! Make yourself at home. We are here to give you the low-down on the organisation – so pay attention!

It's our job to help Da Vinci and his colleagues to solve the tough problems they face and we would like you to join us as members of the Academy. Are you up to the challenge?

Da Vinci
Da Vinci is the founder and head of the Brain Academy. He is all seeing, all thinking and all knowing – possibly the cleverest person alive. Nobody has ever actually seen him in the flesh as he communicates only via computer. When Da Vinci receives an emergency call for help, the members of Brain Academy jump into action (and that means you!).

Huxley
Huxley is Da Vinci's right-hand man. Not as clever, but still very smart. He is here to guide you through the missions and offer help and advice. The sensible and reliable face of Brain Academy, Huxley is cool under pressure.

Dr Hood
The mad doctor is the arch-enemy of Da Vinci and Brain Academy. He has set up a rival organisation called D.A.F.T. (which stands for Dull And Feeble Thinkers). Dr Hood and his agents will do anything they can to irritate and annoy the good people of this planet. He is a pain we could do without.

Hilary Kumar
Ms Kumar is the Prime Minister of our country. As the national leader she has a hotline through to the Academy but will only call in an extreme emergency. Confident and strong willed, she is a very tough cookie indeed.

General Cods-Wallop
This highly decorated gentleman (with medals, not wallpaper) is in charge of the armed forces. Most of his success has come from the help of Da Vinci and the Academy rather than the use of his somewhat limited military brain.

Mrs Tiggles
Stella Tiggles is the retired head of the Secret Intelligence service. She is a particular favourite of Da Vinci who treats her as his own mother. Mrs Tiggles' faithful companion is her cat, Bond… James Bond.

We were just like you once – ordinary schoolchildren leading ordinary lives. Then one day we all received a call from a strange character named Da Vinci. From that day on, we have led a double life – as secret members of Brain Academy!

Here are a few things you should know about the people you'll meet on your journey.

Inspector Pattern
The trusty Inspector is Buster's right-hand lady. Ms Pattern looks for clues in data and is the complete opposite to the muddled D.A.F.T. agents. Using her mathematical mind to find order where there is chaos, she is a welcome addition to Da Vinci's team. In fact some of the team would do well to think in such a methodical way… a certain Mr Blastov perhaps?

Maryland T. Wordsworth
M.T. Wordsworth is the president of the USA. Not the sharpest tool in the box, Maryland prefers to be known by his middle name, Texas, or 'Tex' for short. He takes great exception to being referred to as 'Mary' (which has happened in the past).

Buster Crimes
Buster is a really smooth dude and is in charge of the Police Force. His laid-back but efficient style has won him many friends, although these don't include Dr Hood or the agents of D.A.F.T. who regularly try to trick the coolest cop in town.

Sandy Buckett
The fearless Sandy Buckett is the head of the fire service. Sandy and her team of brave firefighters are always on hand, whether to extinguish the flames of chaos caused by the demented Dr Hood or just to rescue Mrs Tiggles' cat…

Echo the Eco-Warrior
Echo is the hippest chick around. Her love of nature and desire for justice will see her do anything to help an environmental cause – even if it means she's going to get her clothes dirty.

Victor Blastov
Victor Blastov is the leading scientist at the Space Agency. He once tried to build a rocket by himself but failed to get the lid off the glue. Victor often requires the services of the Academy, even if it's to set the video to record Dr Who.

Prince Barrington
Prince Barrington, or 'Bazza' as he is known to his friends, is the publicity-seeking heir to the throne. Always game for a laugh, the Prince will stop at nothing to raise money for worthy causes. A 'good egg' as his mother might say.

Working with Brain Academy

Do you get the idea? Now you've had the introduction we are going to show you the best way to use this book.

MISSION FILE 4:3

A sticker situation for Tex

Time: Just before a meeting with nuclear scientists
Place: The Whitehouse

Tex's office has got into a bit of a mess. He asks his personal assistant Isla Putitaway to help him tidy it up.

Shoo t! I've mixed my bubblegum baseball stic! ers and sports stars collection with my g(vernment reports on that new nuclear p wer station. I'm gonna need a little assis ance here. If you can sort the stickers into the correct albums, I'll be left with the go ernment reports. Am I sharp or what?

About as sharp as a box full of cotton wool! Team, we'd better help Isla tackle this mess.

TM

Stickers: 18, 32, 30, 25, 16, 6, 26, 5, 15, 60

1) Tex asks Isla to put all stickers numbered with a multiple of 5 into the green album. Which stickers go into the green album?

TM

2) Tex changes his mind and starts again. This time, he asks Isla to put all the stickers numbered with a multiple of 6 into the album. Which stickers go into the green album this time?

3) Isla noticed that some stickers went into the green album both times when she sorted them.
   a) Which stickers went in both times?
   b) Why did that happen?

4) a) Write another number that would have gone into the green album both times Isla sorted the stickers.
   b) Explain how you chose the number.

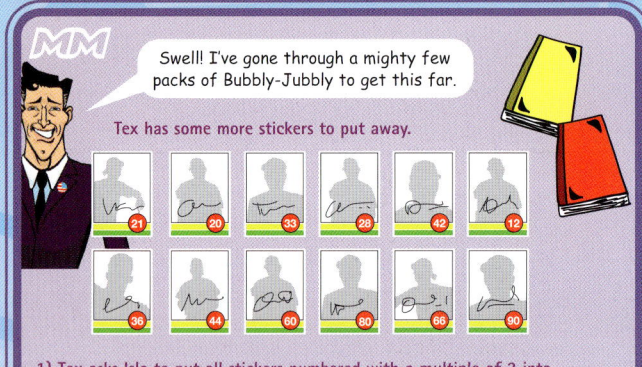

MM

Swell! I've gone through a mighty few packs of Bubbly-Jubbly to get this far.

Tex has some more stickers to put away.

Stickers: 21, 20, 33, 28, 42, 12, 36, 44, 60, 80, 66, 90

1) Tex asks Isla to put all stickers numbered with a multiple of 3 into the yellow album. Which stickers should go into the yellow album?

2) He then asks Isla to put all stickers numbered with a multiple of 4 into the red album. Which stickers should go into the red album?

Each mission is divided up into different parts.

The plot
This tells you what the mission is about.

The Training Mission
Huxley will give you some practice before sending you on the main mission.

Each book contains a number of 'missions' for you to take part in. You will work with the characters in Brain Academy to complete these missions.

Huxley's Think Tank
Huxley will give you some useful tips to help you on each mission.

The Main Mission
This is where you try to complete the challenge.

MM
3) Isla says she doesn't know what to do with some of the stickers.
   a) Which stickers do you think are causing her a problem?
   b) Why do you think that?

4) Here are 4 more stickers that would cause the same problem. Unfortunately, you can only see the number on the top one.

   What numbers could be on the other 3 stickers? Make sure they aren't numbers that have already been used.

HUXLEY'S THINK TANK
Did you know...
- If the digits of a number add up to a multiple of 3, the number itself will be a multiple of 3.
- If a number is a multiple of 4, you can halve it and halve it again and get a whole number answer.

5) Tex has some badges that need sorting, too. This is his red set.

   17 10 15 20 14 25 33 21

   He wants Isla to arrange them so that no two badges next to each other are multiples of the same number, other than being multiples of 1 (which all whole numbers must be).

   So Isla can't put **10** and **15** next to each other as they are both multiples of 5, but she can put **10** and **21** next to each other because they are not multiples of any same number other than 1.

   a) Find a way of arranging the badges.
   b) Can you find a different way of arranging the badges? Don't just reverse the order!

MM
6) Find at least 2 ways of arranging Tex's blue badges so that no two badges next to each other are multiples of the same number other than 1.

   27 24 35 39 61 90 25 47 48 28

7) Make up your own set of 10 badges so that no two badges next to each other are multiples of the same number other than 1.

8) Isla has done so much sorting for Tex that she is getting quite keen on multiples herself!

   She wants to arrange the numbered beads in this bracelet so that no bead next to another bead is a multiple of the same number other than 1.

   Show 1 way of doing this.

   (Beads: 75, 55, 33, 40, 27, 53, 63, 32, 29, 56, 21, 64, 80, 49)

9) Make up your own set of numbered beads so that no two beads next to each other are multiples of the same number other than 1.

Gee, thanks for all your help. I know those 'nuclear' guys collect stickers, too. I wonder if any of them have got any swaps? I've got 12 copies of Willie Socket from the Biffalo Bulls to trade!

Da Vinci files
- Tex has 200 key tags numbered from 1 to 200. He asks Isla to put all the tags that are NOT multiples of either 2 or 5 into a box.
  How many key tags go into the box?

No one said this was easy. In fact, that is why you have been chosen. Da Vinci will only take the best and he believes that includes you. Good luck!

PS: See pages 44–47 for some hints and tips and a useful process.

The Da Vinci Files
These problems are for the best Brain Academy recruits. Very tough. Are you tough enough?

MISSION FILE 4:1

Hose in the house?

Time: To refit the fire station
Place: The fire station office

Sandy Buckett needs to order some new equipment for the fire service. She is comparing prices from a few suppliers. Help her make the most of her money.

I'd rather be fighting fires but needs must!

I know you're more used to saving lives, but let's see if Huxley and his team can help you to save pounds today!

TM

Give Sandy a hand with these hosey posers.

Sandy is buying 2 sizes of hose for 1 fire engine. The hoses are supplied in lengths that fit together. She has written down the prices from 2 suppliers:

Hoses R Us
Small diameter hose: £28 for each 20 m section
Large diameter hose: £47 for each 20 m section

Squirtalot
Small diameter hose: £23 for each 15 m section
Large diameter hose: £34 for each 15 m section

TM

1) She needs 60 m of the smaller hose.
   a) How many sections of hose would she need to buy from Hoses R Us?
   b) How much would the hose cost from Hoses R Us?
   c) How many sections would she need to buy from Squirtalot?
   d) How much would it cost from Squirtalot?
   e) How much will Sandy save by buying the cheaper hose?

2) She needs 120 m of the larger hose.
   a) How many sections would she need to buy from Hoses R Us?
   b) How much would it cost from Hoses R Us?
   c) How many sections would she need to buy from Squirtalot?
   d) How much would the hose cost from Squirtalot?
   e) How much will Sandy save by buying the cheaper hose?

MM

Hmm... these calculations are getting more out of control than Dr Hood! More help please!

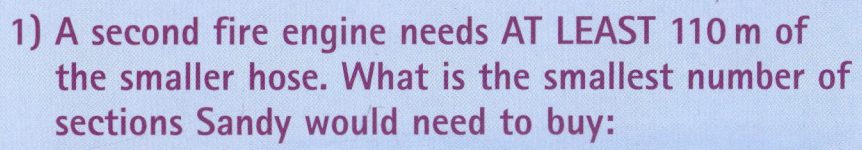

1) A second fire engine needs AT LEAST 110 m of the smaller hose. What is the smallest number of sections Sandy would need to buy:
   a) from Hoses R Us?   b) from Squirtalot?

2) What would the hose cost:
   a) from Hoses R Us?   b) from Squirtalot?

3) How much will Sandy save by buying the cheaper hose?

4) She also needs to buy AT LEAST 175 m of the larger hose for this fire engine.
   a) Which supplier will be cheapest?
   b) How much will Sandy save by buying the cheaper hose?

5) A third fire engine needs EXACTLY 250 m of the smaller hose. To get the length, Sandy has to buy some 15 m sections from Squirtalot and some 20 m sections from Hoses R Us.

   a) What is the least 250 m of the smaller hose could cost?

   b) What is the most 250 m of smaller hose could cost?

6) The third fire engine also needs EXACTLY 350 m of the larger hose. What is the least that Sandy could pay for 330 m of the larger hose?

HUXLEY'S THINK TANK
- Try different combinations of lengths to make the total length you need.
- You might find it helpful to make a list of the lengths that are possible with each of the sizes and see which ones make the totals you need.

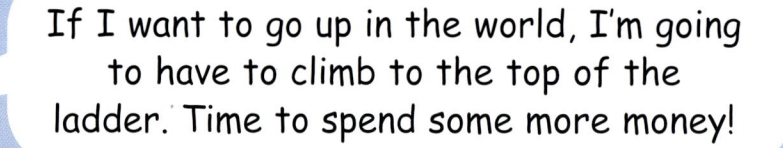

If I want to go up in the world, I'm going to have to climb to the top of the ladder. Time to spend some more money!

7) One type of ladder Sandy wants to buy has the top and bottom rung 25 cm from the ends of the ladder and all the other rungs 30 cm apart.

   a) How long will a ladder with 11 rungs be?

   b) How many rungs will a 5-metre ladder have?

MM

8) The ladders cost £2.80 for each rung plus £1.25 per metre for each side piece.

   So, this rather short ladder would cost £16.80 for the rungs and 4 × £1.25 for the side pieces.

   a) Explain why the rungs would cost £16.80
   b) Explain why the side pieces would cost 4 × £1.25
   c) What is the total cost of the ladder?

9) How much would an 8-metre ladder cost?

25 cm
30 cm
25 cm

I think Sandy has 'rung' the last bit of value from her budget!

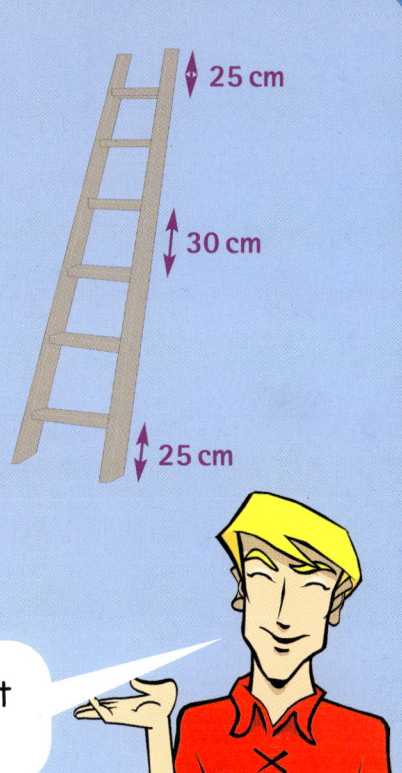

Da Vinci files

- The water tank on the fire engine holds 1,350 l of water. The small hose can pump 100 l of water every minute. How long would it take the small hose to empty the water tank on the fire engine?

- The large hose can pump 1,200 l of water every minute. How many litres is that every second? How long would it take the large hose to empty the water tank on the fire engine?

- The fire engine can also connect to a fire hydrant and pump water from the main water supply, which is a good job really – especially when the large hose is needed!

MISSION FILE 4:2

Happy birthday, Victor!

Time: To put the oven on
Place: Mrs Tiggles' kitchen

It's Victor's birthday and dear old Mrs Tiggles is making him a cake.

That young boy has a sweet tooth. I'm going to surprise him with my special carrot cake. It has 24 carrots in it to help him see in the dark! Can you help me, my dears?

TM: *Start off by helping Mrs Tiggles to weigh out the ingredients.*

When she bakes a cake, Mrs Tiggles still uses her old kitchen balance to weigh out the ingredients.

Most of her weights are marked in OUNCES. Ounces are shown as 'oz' on the weights.

1 oz   2 oz   4 oz   8 oz   1 lb   2 lb

Her 3 largest weights are marked in POUNDS. Pounds are shown as 'lb' on the weights. One pound weighs the same as 16 ounces.
1 lb = 16 oz

4 lb

Remember, Mrs Tiggles has only 1 weight of each size.

TM

1) Mrs Tiggles is making her 24-carrot cake. She used the 1 oz and 2 oz weights to weigh out 3 oz of butter. List the weights she will put on her balance to weigh out:

   a) 12 oz flour
   b) 9 oz mixed chopped nuts
   c) 10 oz of sugar
   d) 7 oz raisins
   e) 14 oz of baby carrots
   e) 11 oz icing sugar

   Each weight can only be used once for each item she has to weigh out.

MM

1) If Mrs Tiggles only uses her ounce weights, the largest amount she can weigh out is 15 oz. That's why the pound weight is needed for 16 oz.

   a) List the weights she would use to make each weight from 1 oz to 1 lb.
   b) List the weights she would use for all the weights between 16 oz and 24 oz.
   c) What weights would she use to weigh out 50 oz?

2) When Mrs Tiggles weighed out some apricots, she used just 2 of her weights. The apricots weighed no more than 20 oz. What weight of apricots could she have weighed out?

3) When she weighed out some margarine, she used 3 of her weights. What weights of margarine up to $2\frac{1}{2}$ lbs could she NOT have weighed out?

HUXLEY'S THINK TANK

- Sometimes it is helpful to find out what you can do so that you can find out what you can't do! So, when finding weights that can't be made, it might be a good idea to start off by finding the ones that can be made.

MM

When the cake is ready, Mrs Tiggles takes it to Victor Blastov at the Space Agency. She finds him working on an old computer. Instead of having a screen, the computer sends its results out on punched paper tape.

That paper tape reminds me of the weights I used to make my cake!

Vot do you mean?

The holes are arranged in columns that use the same values as my weights, but with the pounds shown in ounces!

This is 10 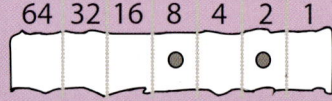 — which would use 8 oz, 2 oz

This is 39 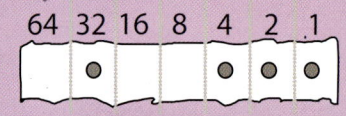 — which would use 2 lb, 4 oz, 2 oz, 1 oz

4) a) What number is this? 
   b) What weights would make the same number?

5) a) What number is this? 
   b) What weights would make the same number?

6) a) What number is this? 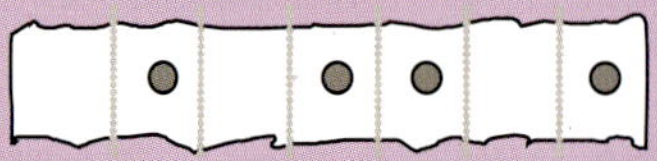
   b) What weights would make the same number?

7) Show how these numbers would be made using paper tape. You might want to use squared paper to help with the columns.

   a) 19   b) 4   c) 57   d) 75   e) 80   f) 100

Now, I'll let you into my secret Mrs T. Zis paper tape says 'cake'! I vos going to send you a secret message to bake a cake vich couldn't be intercepted by zos D.A.F.T. agents!

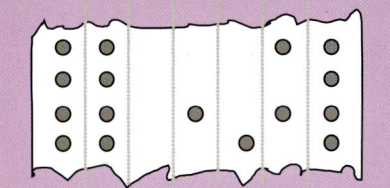

Really Victor, you are a clever boy.

Ja! Look at zis code used by my computer to give a number to each letter.

Letter	a	b	c	d	e	f	g	h	i	j	k	l	m
Code	97	98	99	100	101	102	103	104	105	106	107	108	109

Letter	n	o	p	q	r	s	t	u	v	w	x	y	z
Code	110	111	112	113	114	115	116	117	118	119	120	121	122

8) Can you work out how Victor's paper tape says 'cake'?

9) What does this paper tape say?

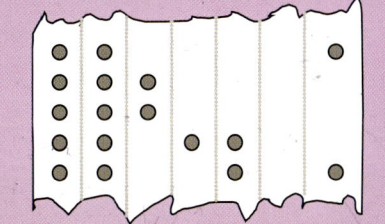

10) Draw a paper tape that says 'yoghurt'.

Da Vinci files

- In the code, capital letters use the numbers that are 32 less than the numbers shown in the table.

    e.g. **a** is 97   97 − 32 = 65   so   65 is the code for capital **A**

    p is 112   112 − 32 = 80   so   80 is the code for capital **P**

    Draw the paper tape that says 'VICTOR'.

- What letter would 'weigh' 5 lb 8 oz using Mrs Tiggles' weights?

MISSION FILE 4:3

A sticker situation for Tex

Time: Just before a meeting with nuclear scientists
Place: The Whitehouse

Tex's office has got into a bit of a mess. He asks his personal assistant Isla Putitaway to help him tidy it up.

Shoot! I've mixed my bubblegum baseball stickers and sports stars collection with my government reports on that new nuclear power station. I'm gonna need a little assistance here. If you can sort the stickers into the correct albums, I'll be left with the government reports. Am I sharp or what?

About as sharp as a box full of cotton wool Team, we'd better help Isla tackle this mess.

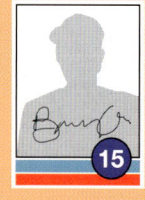

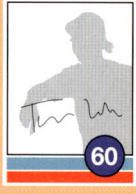

TM

18 32 30 25 16

24 26 6 15 60

1) Tex asks Isla to put all stickers numbered with a multiple of 5 into the green album. Which stickers go into the green album?

TM

2) Tex changes his mind and starts again. This time, he asks Isla to put all the stickers numbered with a multiple of 6 into the album. Which stickers go into the green album this time?

3) Isla noticed that some stickers went into the green album both times when she sorted them.

   a) Which stickers went in both times?

   b) Why did that happen?

4) a) Write another number that would have gone into the green album both times Isla sorted the stickers.

   b) Explain how you chose the number.

MM

Swell! I've gone through a mighty few packs of Bubbly-Jubbly to get this far.

Tex has some more stickers to put away.

Stickers: 21, 20, 33, 28, 42, 12, 36, 44, 60, 80, 66, 90

1) Tex asks Isla to put all stickers numbered with a multiple of 3 into the yellow album. Which stickers should go into the yellow album?

2) He then asks Isla to put all stickers numbered with a multiple of 4 into the red album. Which stickers should go into the red album?

3) Isla says she doesn't know what to do with some of the stickers.

   a) Which stickers do you think are causing her a problem?

   b) Why do you think that?

4) Here are 4 more stickers that would cause the same problem. Unfortunately, you can only see the number on the top one.

   What numbers could be on the other 3 stickers? Make sure they aren't numbers that have already been used.

HUXLEY'S THINK TANK

Did you know...

- If the digits of a number add up to a multiple of 3, the number itself will be a multiple of 3.
- If a number is a multiple of 4, you can halve it and halve it again and get a whole number answer.

5) Tex has some badges that need sorting, too. This is his red set.

   17   10   15   20   14   25   33   21

   He wants Isla to arrange them so that no two badges next to each other are multiples of the same number, other than being multiples of 1 (which all whole numbers must be).

   So Isla can't put **10** and **15** next to each other as they are both multiples of 5, but she can put **10** and **21** next to each other because they are not multiples of any same number other than 1.

   a) Find a way of arranging the badges.

   b) Can you find a different way of arranging the badges? Don't just reverse the order!

6) Find at least 2 ways of arranging Tex's blue badges so that no two badges next to each other are multiples of the same number other than 1.

27 24 35 39 61 90 25 47 48 28

7) Make up your own set of 10 badges so that no two badges next to each other are multiples of the same number other than 1.

8) Isla has done so much sorting for Tex that she is getting quite keen on multiples herself!

She wants to arrange the numbered beads in this bracelet so that no bead next to another bead is a multiple of the same number other than 1.

Show 1 way of doing this.

9) Make up your own set of numbered beads so that no two beads next to each other are multiples of the same number other than 1.

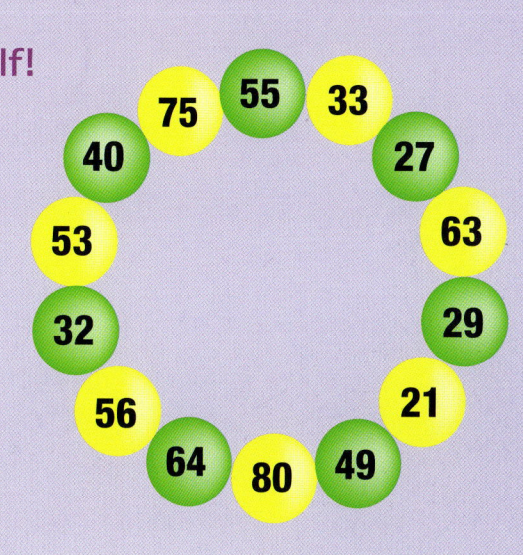

Bracelet beads: 75, 55, 33, 40, 27, 53, 63, 32, 29, 56, 21, 64, 80, 49

Gee, thanks for all your help. I know those 'nuclear' guys collect stickers, too. I wonder if any of them have got any swaps? I've got 12 copies of Willie Socket from the Biffalo Bulls to trade!

Da Vinci Files

- Tex has 200 key tags numbered from 1 to 200. He asks Isla to put all the tags that are NOT multiples of either 2 or 5 into a box.

  How many key tags go into the box?

MISSION FILE 4:4

Fractious fractions

Time: After reading the morning papers
Place: Hilary Kumar's office

FRY

The FRYs (Fractional Rights Yobs) are demanding that instead of decimals, fractions are used to display information. Hilary Kumar asks advice from the Brain Academy.

Fractious fraction faction action... we need some explanations before the country panics...

Hilary's right. Help Huxley get some information out to the public – quickly!

TM

Sometimes fractions use larger numbers than they need.

1) Show Ms Kumar that some fractions can be simplified by writing these fractions in their simplest form:

   a) $\frac{4}{20}$ b) $\frac{6}{8}$ c) $\frac{15}{45}$ d) $\frac{18}{27}$

2) Decimals and fractions show the same information.

   a) BA agents spend $\frac{7}{10}$ths of their time in training. What is $\frac{7}{10}$ths as a decimal? Use your calculator to divide 7 by 10. What answer do you get?

   b) One third of Dr Hood's spies think the hidden camera is the one in their pocket!

   What do you think $\frac{1}{3}$ is as a decimal? Use your calculator to check if you are correct.

c) Da Vinci receives $\frac{7}{20}$ths of the reports at BA headquarters.
What do you think $\frac{7}{20}$ is as a decimal?
Use your calculator to check if you are correct.

3) a) BA spends 0.5 of their money designing new gadgets.
What is 0.5 as a fraction?
Use your calculator to see if the fraction you wrote is the same as 0.5.

b) 0.6 of the BA workforce speak at least 2 languages.
What do you think 0.6 is as a fraction? Explain why you think that.

c) 0.75 of the BA missions are completed on time.
What is 0.75 as a fraction? Use your calculator to see if the fraction you wrote is the same as 0.75.

d) Da Vinci signs 0.92 of the BA paperwork. No wonder we never see him!
What do you think 0.92 is as a fraction? Explain why you think that.

HUXLEY'S THINK TANK

$$1/3 = 0.3333333...$$

- When a decimal number keeps repeating like the one above, we say it is RECURRING.
- We can write it with a recurring dot over the number that is repeated, like this: $0.\dot{3}$

4) a) Write 0.666666666... as a recurring decimal.

b) What does $0.\dot{9}$ mean?

5) Write down the decimal equivalents of the fraction family of fifths.
Explain any patterns you find.

$\frac{1}{5}$ $\frac{2}{5}$ $\frac{3}{5}$ $\frac{4}{5}$ $\frac{5}{5}$

Hilary vants me to investigate zees decimals a bit more... vot vill happen if I use a calculator, I vonder? Technology ees magnificent!

1) Victor Blastov divided 1 by a number on his calculator. His calculator showed 0.11111111111

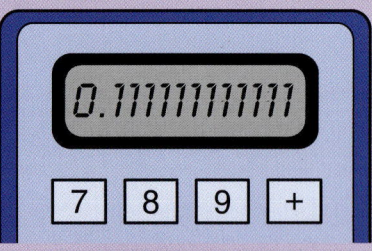

   Use your calculator to find out what number he divided by.

2) Victor keeps dividing by the same number.
   a) What happens when he divides 2 by the number?
   b) What happens when he divides 3 by the number?
   c) What do you think will happen if he divides 4 by the number? Predict before you try on your calculator.
   d) What if he divides 5 by the number? Predict before trying.
   e) How far does this pattern carry on?
   f) Investigate what happens if you divide 10, 11, 12 and so on by the same number. Does your rule still work? If not, how do you need to change it?

3) Now look at this decimal number.

   0.09090909...

   It was also made by dividing 1 by a number.
   a) What is the number that 1 was divided by to make this decimal?
   b) Try dividing other numbers by that number. Look for a pattern.
   c) Explain the pattern in the decimal numbers and give a rule for changing these decimals to fractions.

4) a) Find the fraction that is equivalent to $0.05\dot{5}$?
   b) Look at some other fractions in this group. Explain any pattern you find in their decimal equivalents.

5) Some fractions have longer recurring patterns when they are changed to decimals.

   a) Find the smallest fraction with a recurring pattern of 6 digits in the equivalent decimal.

   b) Investigate the decimal numbers equivalent to this family of fractions. Explain any patterns you find.

You'll need a calculator with a 12-digit display. You could try using the calculator on your computer.

Those FRYs have totally 'missed the point'... thanks team, for a great result!

Da Vinci Files

- Exchange rates are shown as decimals. Look in the newspaper or on the internet for today's exchange rates.
- Exchange rates only belong to fraction families if there is a repeating pattern in the decimal number. Can you find any exchange rates which belong to fraction families? What are they?

  Record your findings clearly in both decimal and fractional forms, remembering to write both of the currencies used.
- Look for exchange rates that are as close as possible to the fraction family of ninths.

  Which members of the fraction families can you find?
- Estimate fractions for other exchange rates and then use your calculator to change your fractions to decimals. How close was your estimate? Try other exchange rates and see if your estimates become more accurate.

MISSION FILE 4:5

Spot the sausage!

```
Time: After dinner
Place: The ballroom,
Barrington Hall
```

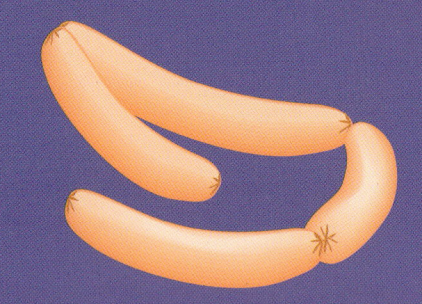

Prince Barrington is raising money for another charity – C.H.U.N.D.E.R. (Children United Against Dodgy Educational Reforms). He is running a sort of 'spot the ball' competition... but with sausages... 'Hot dog!' as the royal fruit cake might say.

A marvellously warm welcome to Barrington Hall! Sausages ahoy, what?

Ahem. Still all in the name of charity, eh Prince?

TM

To make the competition fair, I've come up with some rules.

- The sausage is buried at a secret position on the map.
- Draw lines on the map so that they cross wherever you think the sausage might be buried.
- You can only draw straight lines.
- You can draw as many lines as you like.
- Each line you draw costs 10p.

The winner is the player whose lines cross nearest to the position of the buried sausage.

1) What is the least you would have to pay to have a chance of winning?

2) General Cods-Wallop paid 30p and drew these 3 lines that made 2 crossings.

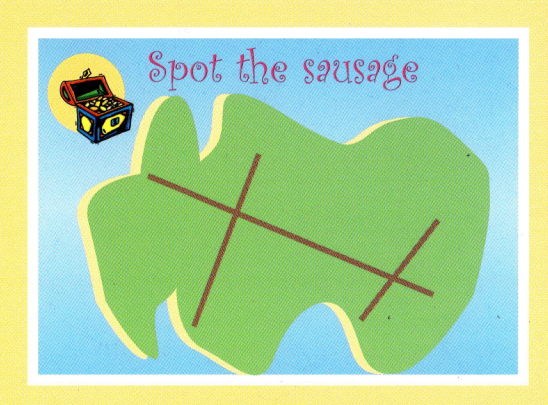

Spot the sausage

Oh General! You could make more crossings than that with three lines. The more crossings you have, the more likely you are to win.

How could the General draw 3 straight lines so that he made more crossings?

3) Mrs Tiggles paid 40p and drew these 4 lines on her map.

   a) Could Mrs Tiggles have made more crossings with her 4 straight lines?

   b) What is the largest number of crossings she could make with 4 straight lines?

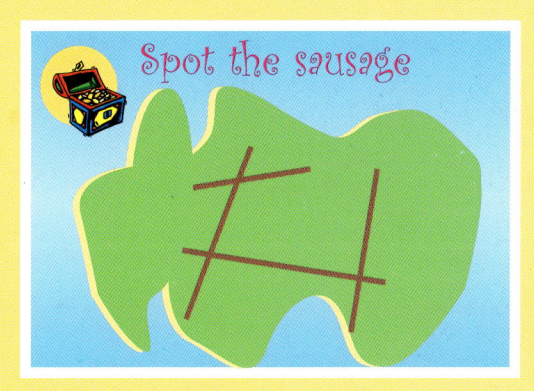

Spot the sausage

HUXLEY'S THINK TANK

- Parallel lines always stay the same distance apart. They don't get closer together or further apart.
- When you are trying to get lines to cross, you don't want to use parallel lines!

25

I've been thinking about the greatest number of crossings that could be made with the different number of lines. I think I can see the start of a pattern...!

1 line makes 0 crossings
2 lines make 1 crossing
3 lines make 3 crossings
4 lines make 6 crossings...

1) What pattern can you see in the numbers?

2) Without drawing anything, predict the greatest number of crossings that can be made using:

   a) 5 lines?   b) 6 lines?

3) Now check your predictions by making a drawing. Were you right?

4) Copy and complete this table showing the greatest number of crossings for different numbers of lines:

Number of lines	Largest number of crossings
1	0
2	1
3	3
4	6
5	
6	

5) 1 cut will give 2 pieces of cake...

2 cuts will give 3 pieces...

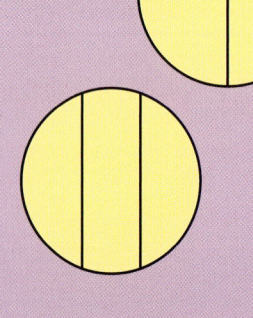

... or 4 pieces.

I think this table might help me with another problem! I've been thinking about how to cut the Prince's celebration cake using as few straight cuts as possible.

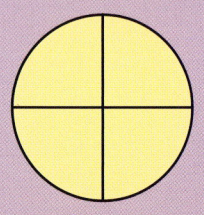

Draw your own cake. What is the largest number of pieces you can get using 3 straight cuts? The pieces don't have to be the same size as each other.

MM 6) Draw another cake. What is the largest number of pieces you can get using 4 straight cuts?

7) a) Copy this table and fill in the number of pieces for 3 and 4 cuts.

Number of cuts	Largest number of pieces
0	1
1	2
2	4
3	
4	

b) What pattern can you see in the numbers?

c) Why does Inspector Pattern think the 'Spot the sausage' competition will help her find the pattern?

Look at the tables from questions 4 and 7 to help you!

8) Without drawing, predict the largest number of pieces of cake you will get with:

a) 5 cuts   b) 6 cuts

Check your predictions by making a drawing. Start with a large circle.

Bangers 'n' cash – the perfect dish for my charity pals!

Da Vinci files

- Hilary Kumar played just 1 game of 'Spot the sausage'. She made more than 50 crossings. What is the least amount she could have paid for her game?
- Sandy Buckett spent £1.50 on 'Spot the sausage'. What is the largest number of crossings she could make?
- There were between 80 and 90 people at the royal ball. What is the smallest number of cuts Inspector Pattern could make for everyone to have a piece of cake?

MISSION FILE 4:6

Per cent per chance?

Time: To get a grip!
Place: Da Vinci's morning briefing

Keeping track of all the Missions and the Academy teams on each one, as well as Dr Hood's dodgy dealings and his agents of silliness, is proving to be a struggle even for Da Vinci's mighty brain. He's called Huxley in to help clear his memory... and his headache!

I've been giving some thought to this, sir, and I think we can use percentages to make the figures easier to work with.

Sounds like a plan to me! Time to rouse the team into action...

TM

Let's warm up by giving these facts and figures as percentages.

1) Write the percentage for each of the statements.

a) There is a 40 out of 100 chance that Dr Hood has contacted hostile aliens.

b) There are 73 out of 100 aliens with special powers.

c) There are 55 out of 100 aliens with 3 eyes as well as x-ray vision.

d) There are 4 out of 10 aliens who want to increase trade with the planet Earth.

e) Trade is problem free in 2 out of 5 cases.

f) Da Vinci has information about 18 out of every 20 alien races.

Now, can you give me some more help here?

2) Using cm-squared paper, draw 1 rectangle with an area of 10 cm² and another with an area of 20 cm².

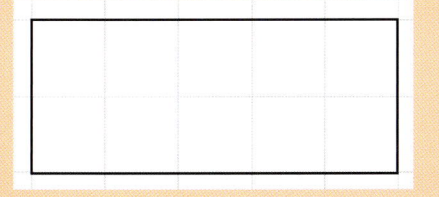

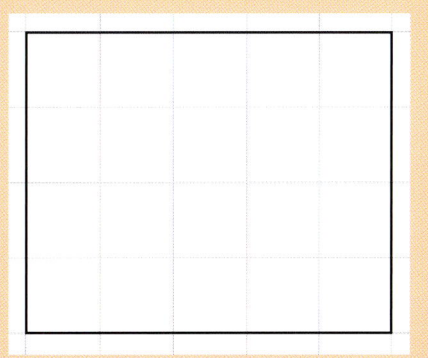

   a) Colour 10% of each rectangle. How many squares did you need to colour in each rectangle?

   b) How many squares do you think it takes to colour 10% of a rectangle with an area of 30 cm²? Now work it out for a rectangle 40 cm².

   Check your answers by drawing the rectangles.

   c) Can you find a rule for finding 10% of a number? Explain your rule.

   d) 300 agents meet at the base. 10% are sent on missions.
   205 catch a mystery illness and go home.

   Use your rule to work out how many agents are left at the base.

3) Use the same rectangles as question 2 and colour 20% of each one.

   a) Compare the sizes of the rectangles and the number of squares you needed to colour. Can you spot any patterns?

   b) Explain what you find, then work out a rule for finding 20% of a number.

   c) Use your rule to work out this problem for Echo.

   There are 500 uniforms.
   20% are being washed.
   10% are being worn.
   12% are lost.

   How many are left in the cupboard?

Copy this table and use your results so far to complete it.

Area of rectangle	Number of squares you need to colour to make			
	10%	20%	30%	40%
10 cm²				
20 cm²				
30 cm²				
40 cm²				
50 cm²				

1) Explain the patterns you find in these results and use your explanations to write instructions for quick ways of finding 30%, 40% and 50%. Which multiplications would get the same answers?

Look for patterns in your results.

2) Use your rules and instructions to find these answers at top speed.

Number of agents	Number of agents needed for			
	10%	20%	30%	40%
60 agents				
70 agents				
90 agents				
100 agents				
300 agents				

3) Look at the rules you have found for finding different percentages. Try to spot patterns in your rules. What do you think the rule for finding 70% might be?

4) Buster Crimes finds 700 identity cards. 3 get lost and 7 are damaged.

Of the rest, 90% are genuine. How many fakes does that leave?

Excellent! Now, let's get these problems out of the way.

MM

5) Da Vinci gets 240 letters in the post. Of them, 60% are bills and 10% are letters of complaint. The others are requests for help.

How many requests for help are there?

Good work team. I'll give you all 95% for effort!

Da Vinci files

- A maximum of 10% of aliens from the planet Plop visit the Brain Academy every year. Last year, 20 aliens visited. What is the possible range of the population of Plop?

HUXLEY'S THINK TANK
- You need to work out the maximum and minimum values!

- A minimum of 80% of all the alien guests use the visitors' gate. If 400 aliens use the visitors' gate, what is the possible range of the total number of alien visitors?

- Now create a similar problem of your own. Use a maximum of 20% and have the answer range 5 to 50. Check that your problem works!

MISSION FILE 4:7

The truth is out there...

Time: Prime time
Place: Victor's lab

Victor Blastov needs some special numbers for a formula he is working out. He is preparing a truth potion to be given to Dr Hood's spies when they are caught.

"Huxley, find the prime candidates for this mission."

"I need ze numbers quickly. Ze formula must be finished today."

"I've considered all the factors and I'm handing this mission to the perfect group."

TM

"Victor Blastov needs some prime numbers sorting straight away. Complete your training mission so he can continue with his potion."

1 a) Identify all the prime numbers between 1 and 50.

HUXLEY'S THINK TANK
- Remember, prime numbers have only TWO factors.

b) Explain why the number 2 is the only even prime number.

2) Use this example to help you answer the following questions.

> **Factors of 12**
> 1 × 12 = 12
> ②× 6 = 12
> ③× 4 = 12
> So, the factors of 12 are 1, 2, 3, 4, 6 and 12.

2 and 3 are the prime factors of 12.

Find all the factors of
a) 8   b) 15   c) 24
d) 30   e) 23   f) 36

Circle the prime numbers in each list of factors.

3) Now use this example to help you answer these questions.

> **Making 12 using prime factors**
> 2 × 2 × 3 = 12

Prime factors are the most effective numbers!

Write these numbers as products of prime factors.
a) 15   b) 24   c) 30
d) 40   e) 45   f) 63

4) Find the smallest numbers with these prime factors:
a) 5 and 2   b) 3, 5 and 2
c) 3 and 7   d) 7, 11 and 12
e) 13 and 3   f) 17, 3 and 2

1) Victor investigates square numbers as a product of their prime factors. He finds that:

> 2 × 2 = 4
> 3 × 3 = 9
> 2 × 2 × 2 × 2 = 16

Victor thinks that square numbers just have 1 prime factor.
Is he right? Explain your answer.

2) The number 30 has 3 different prime factors:

> 30 = 2 × 3 × 5

Find the other number less than 50, which has 3 different prime factors.

These numbers are part of the prime family of 3 because they have 3 different prime factors.

3) Find numbers between 50 and 100, which are members of the prime family of 3.

4) a) Find the smallest number that is a member of the prime family of 4.

   b) What is the smallest number that is a member of the prime family of 5?

5) Write all the numbers between 1 and 100 that have only 1 prime factor.

> Start with the lowest prime number. Keep multiplying it by itself and make all the numbers you can that are less than 100.

> Do the same thing with the other prime numbers... Victor needs them quickly to complete the truth serum...

"I'm trying out ze potion. Glug... glug... glug... I'm ze greatest scientific genius zis planet has ever seen!"

"Sigh... Obviously, another of Victor's spectacular failures!"

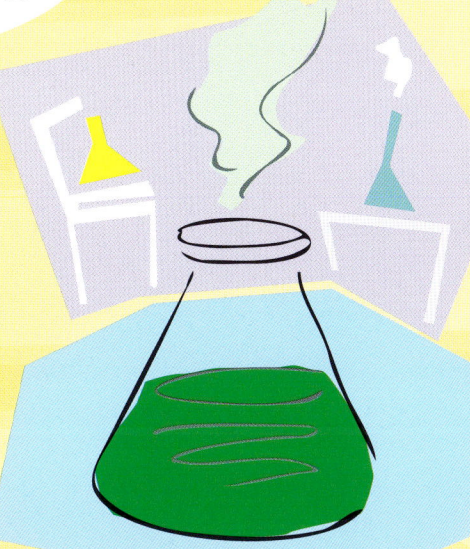

Da Vinci files

2^5

- Find out about the number 5 written next to the number 2. What is it called? What does it do?
- Write all the numbers between 90 and 100 using numbers like this and prime factors.

$$84 = 2^2 \times 3 \times 7$$

MISSION FILE 4:8

Rock on, Buster C!

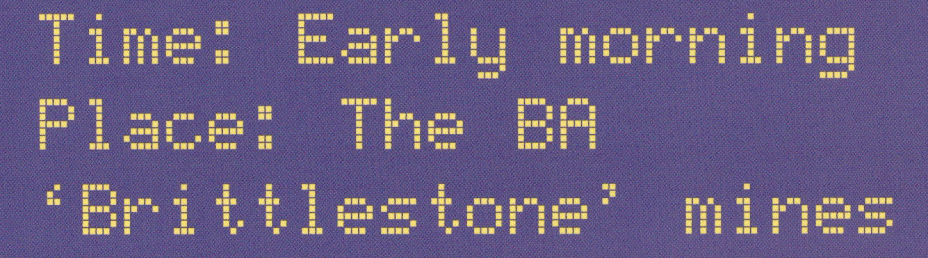

Time: Early morning
Place: The BA 'Brittlestone' mines

'Brittlestone' is very expensive. It comes in many shapes and is mined for its radioactive powers. However… DAFT agents have been breaking off corners of the valuable mineral to steal it for their own half-brained purposes. Buster Crimes wants something done to protect the mineral shapes.

"If I could cover the corners of those mineral shapes with some kinda protective coating, I could stop those rocks from disappearing."

"I might be able to help you out, sir."

"All these different shapes, dude – it'll take hours to work out how much coating I need for each!"

TM

"Let's tackle the triangular shapes first.

1) Draw a triangle and tear off the corners."

Now, stick the corners together.

a) What do you notice?

b) What does this tell you about the 3 angles of the triangle?

2) Try the same thing with a different triangle. What happens? Does the same thing happen with ANY triangle that you try?

Will it happen with right-angled triangles, equilateral triangles, isosceles triangles and scalene triangles?

3) a) What happens if you put the 4 corners of a rectangle together?

b) What does that tell you about the 4 angles of a rectangle?

4) a) Investigate the angle sum of all these quadrilaterals.

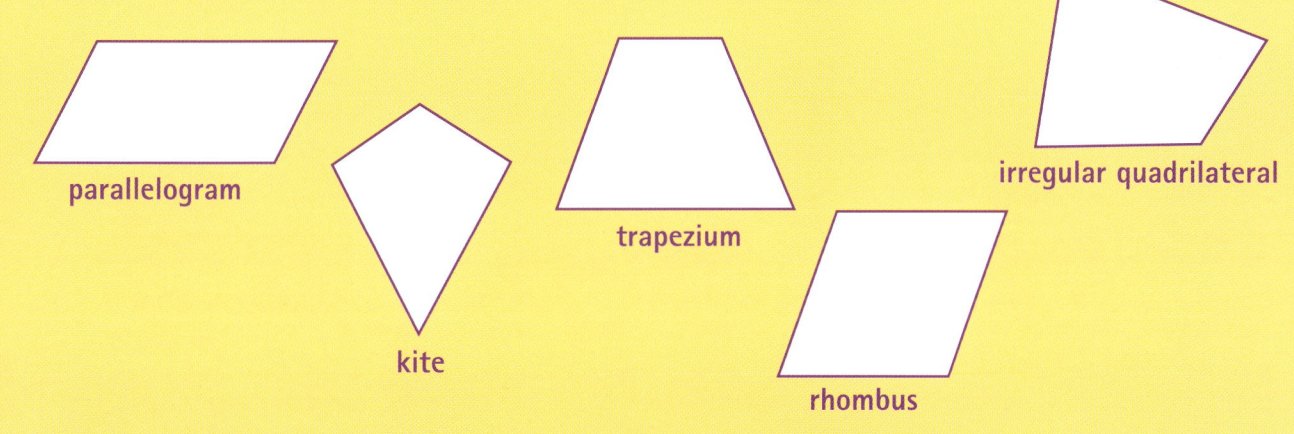

parallelogram

kite

trapezium

rhombus

irregular quadrilateral

b) Investigate the angle sum of some other quadrilaterals. What do you find?

4) You can split a square into 2 triangles.

Find the smallest number of triangles you can split other quadrilaterals into.

Believe me – you want to make the smallest number of triangles you can for this mission.

Hey dude! I could make a whole lot more triangles than that.

"Now for some other shapes."

"Cool! You know, this job is looking easier already."

1) a) Investigate the angle sum of regular and irregular pentagons. You might find this will make more than 1 complete turn.

   b) Draw diagonals onto a pentagon to split it into triangles. What is the smallest number of triangles needed to split the pentagon into triangles?

2) a) Investigate the angle sum of regular and irregular hexagons.

   b) Draw diagonals onto a hexagon to split it into triangles. What is the smallest number of triangles needed to split the hexagon into triangles?

3) a) Investigate the angle sum of regular and irregular heptagons.

   b) Draw diagonals onto a heptagon to split it into triangles. What is the smallest number of triangles needed to split the heptagon into triangles?

4) a) Investigate the angle sum of regular and irregular octagons.

   b) Draw diagonals onto an octagon to split it into triangles. What is the smallest number of triangles needed to split the octagon into triangles?

"Any more rockin' raids and heads are gonna roll!"

MM

5) a) Is there any connection between the angle sum of a shape and the smallest number of triangles it can be split into?

Explain your connection and use it to make a rule that will make it easy to find the angle sum of any polygon.

b) Use your rule to work out the angle sum of a decagon.

Da Vinci files

- a, b and c are the exterior angles of the red triangle. Explain how to draw them.

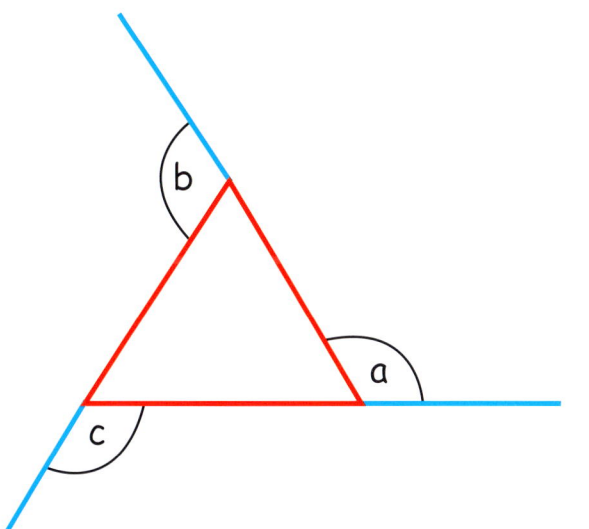

- Find the sum of the exterior angles of the red triangle.
- Investigate the sum of the external angles of different shapes.

Can you find a pattern or a rule for the sum of the external angles of shapes?

MISSION FILE 4:9

What a clever pussy you are, you are... oh what a clever pussy, you are!

Time: Paw o'clock
Place: The local veterinary surgery

Mrs Tiggles took her cat James Bond to the vet for a cat IQ test! He did all sorts of tasks including recognising 124 species of fish, tangling up 53 balls of wool and painting an excellent version of the 'Meowna Lisa'. In fact, he scored a purrrfect ten each time.

Da Vinci, did you hear? The vet said James was smarter than your 'average' cat...

Indeed Mrs T. 'Average', James is certainly not!

I'm still a bit confused though... Who is this Average and why would the vet think I had another cat? James is all the cat I need!

I think it's time we brushed up on your mathematical skills, dear Mrs T! Huxley, can you lead us through some averages?

40

Let's start by measuring data. Different ways of doing this include the mode, median, mean and range.

1) Explain what these measures are and how to work them out.

2) A 3 6 3
   B 2 5 5 1 2
   C 10 12 2 1 4 1
   D 3 4 9 4
   E 10 1 3 2 10 4
   F 3 2 11 7 3 13

   a) Find the range of each of these data sets.
   b) Find the mode of each of these data sets.
   c) Find the median of each of these data sets.
   d) Find the mean of each of these data sets.
   e) Compare your answers for each set.

   What do you notice about the mean, median and mode for each set?

   Are they the same? Explain the reason for this.

   f) Choose one of the sets.
   Remove one of the numbers and work out the mean, median and mode.

   How do they compare to your answers for the original set? Explain the reason for this.

HUXLEY'S THINK TANK

- Remember, if there is an even number of terms in the set, the median is the midpoint between the two middle numbers.

1) The original data for these sets has been lost. 10 is the highest possible term and all the terms are positive integers.

Find the original data set that would work and calculate the mean.

a) mode = 3, median = 3, range = 5, number of terms = 3

> The median is 3 so the middle number is 3. And the mode is 3, so there must be at least one more 3. Hmmm...

3 terms ☐ 3 ☐

b) mode = 8, median = 7, range = 3, there are 5 terms

c) mode = 9, median = 6, range = 4, there are 7 terms

2) There is more than 1 data set that will fit these results. Find all the data sets that give these results.

a) mode = 6, median = 6, range = 2, there are 3 terms

b) mode = 3, median = 5, range = 7, there are 5 terms

c) mode = 5, median = 5, range = 5, there are 4 terms

d) mode = 8, median = 9, range = 6, there are 6 terms

> My dear boy, thinking about averages is making my head ache more than average.

> One last challenge to go, Mrs T, and you'll be our averages queen!

3) Now for the ultimate challenge! Find the sets that will give these results.

   a) mode = 1, median = 3, range = 7, mean = 4, there are 5 terms (1 possible solution)

   b) mode = 9, median = 6, range = 7, mean = 6, there are 6 terms (1 possible solution)

   c) mode = 8, median = 7, range = 10, mean = 5, there are 7 terms (1 possible solution)

   d) mode = 1, median = 5, range = 7, mean = 4, there are 7 terms (2 possible solutions)

James is so clever he would like to study to be a doctor. That would make him a 'first-aid-kit'!

Da Vinci files

- Make up some similar problems.
- Decide how many terms you are going to have.
  - Keeping your terms in order from the smallest to the largest, write in a median term.
  - Next, fill in enough terms to create a mode.
  - Check the total of the terms you have chosen so far and then fill in the other terms so that the total divides by the number of terms to give a whole number for the mean.
- Check that your terms are still in order.
- Write down the mode, median, mean and range and challenge your friends to find a data set that fits the answers.

Mission Strategies

MISSION FILE 4:1

When the Main Mission says that Sandy needs AT LEAST a certain length of hose, if you can't make the length exactly, make sure you buy more than the length she needs – but also that you have the smallest amount of extra hose that you can!

With the questions about the ladders, think about the connection between the number of rungs and the number of gaps between the rungs.

MISSION FILE 4:2

In the Main Mission question 3, you are asked to find the weights that Mrs Tiggles CAN'T weigh out. As the amounts can't be made using her set of weights, you won't be able to make them! So, it might be a good idea to start off by finding all the weights up to $2\frac{1}{2}$ lbs she CAN make – then you should be able to say which weights she can't make.

MISSION FILE 4:3

It can be quite hard to arrange the badges and beads so that no two next to each other are multiples of the same number other than 1, especially with the beads where the ends join up. You might find it helpful to write each number on a scrap of paper and then list all the numbers that it is a multiple of so that you can move the numbers around to find a solution.

MISSION FILE 4:4

To change a fraction to a decimal, divide the numerator (top number) by the denominator (bottom number). When you are searching for a denominator to make a particular fraction, try with low denominators first and work up systematically.

If you can't find exchange rates that convert easily to fractions for the Da Vinci challenge, try to find fractions that are equivalent to the first 2 or 3 numbers after the decimal point. Use mixed numbers for exchange rates that are greater than 1.

MISSION FILE 4:5

When you are drawing lines to make as many crossings as you can, watch out for any crossings where more than 2 lines cross at the same place. If you do find places where more than 2 lines cross, moving 1 or more of the lines across a little bit will make more crossings.

Looking at the differences between the numbers in the tables might help you to spot some patterns.

MISSION FILE 4:6

To work out the percentage, multiply the fractions up until the denominator is 100. Alternatively, convert the fraction to a decimal (look at the strategy for Mission 4) and then multiply the answer by 100.

The patterns should be quite straightforward to find. In the Da Vinci files, take 1% as the minimum amount to find the maximum number and 10% as the number to find the minimum answer.

MISSION FILE 4:7

When you are looking for prime factors of numbers, remember that a prime factor can be repeated. For example, a number with the prime factors 2 and 3 could be 2 x 3 = 6 or 2 x 2 x 3 = 12 or 2 x 3 x 3 x 3 = 54. When you are looking for all the numbers with certain prime factors, start with the smallest prime factors you can and increase the numbers systematically.

MISSION FILE 4:8

Cutting needs to be accurate for this Mission. When you are finding the angle sum, it is a good idea to make a dark dot and make sure all the vertices (corners) touch it. Make sure the sides of the shapes don't overlap.

The minimum number of triangles each shape will divide into has a very important relationship to the angle sum of a shape.

In the Da Vinci files, you could try cutting out the external angles and arranging them around a point to find the angle sum.

MISSION FILE 4:9

When you are trying to find a data set, try to put in the fixed numbers first. Make sure the numbers go in order, usually from the smallest to the largest.

It also helps to work out the sum of the terms. You can do this if you know the mean. For example, if the mean is 4 and there are 5 terms, then the sum of the terms must be 4 x 5 = 20. This will help you work out some of the missing numbers.

The TASC Problem Solving Wheel

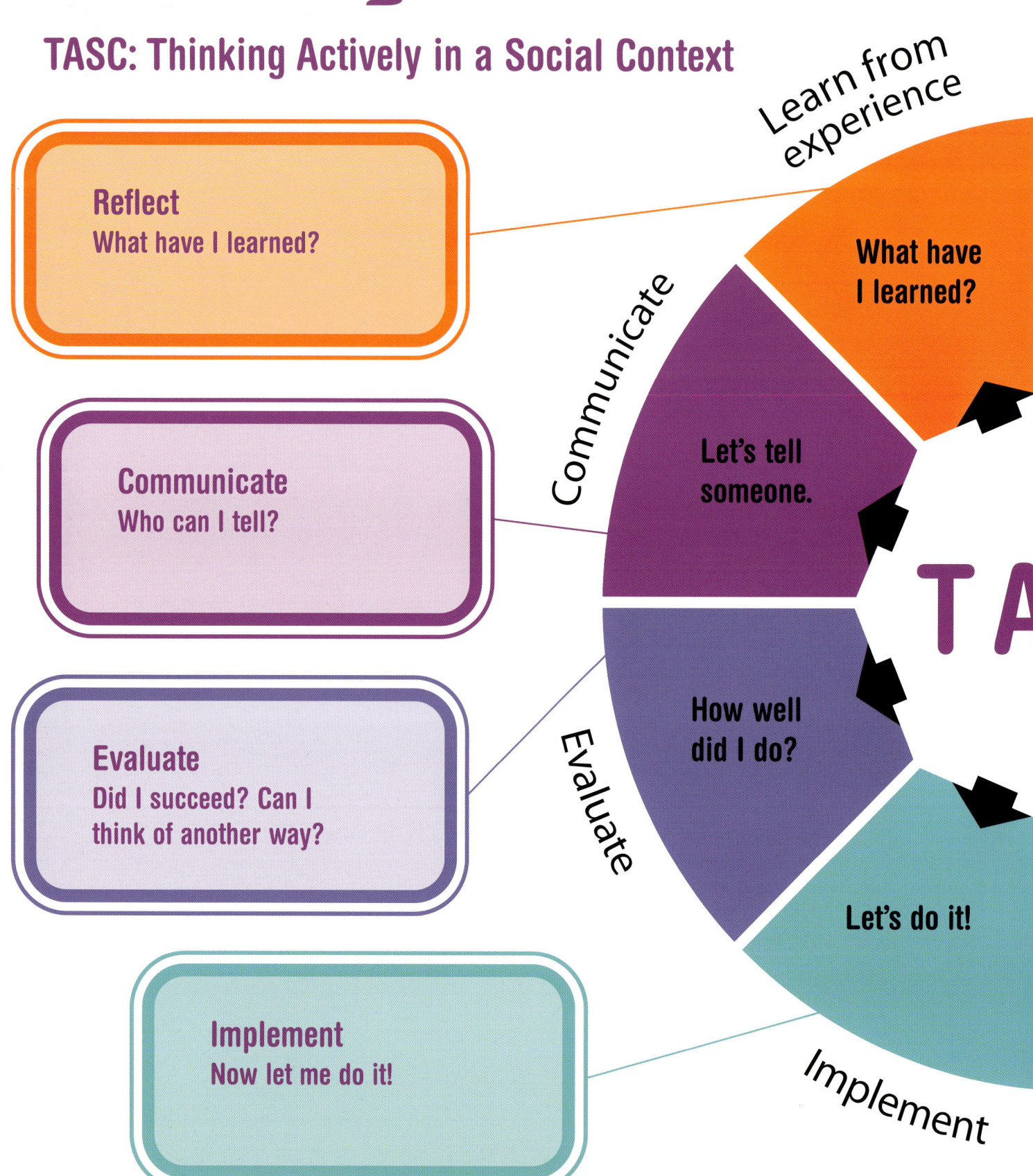

TASC: Thinking Actively in a Social Context

Reflect
What have I learned?

Communicate
Who can I tell?

Evaluate
Did I succeed? Can I think of another way?

Implement
Now let me do it!

Learn from experience — What have I learned?

Communicate — Let's tell someone.

Evaluate — How well did I do?

Implement — Let's do it!

We can learn to be expert thinkers!

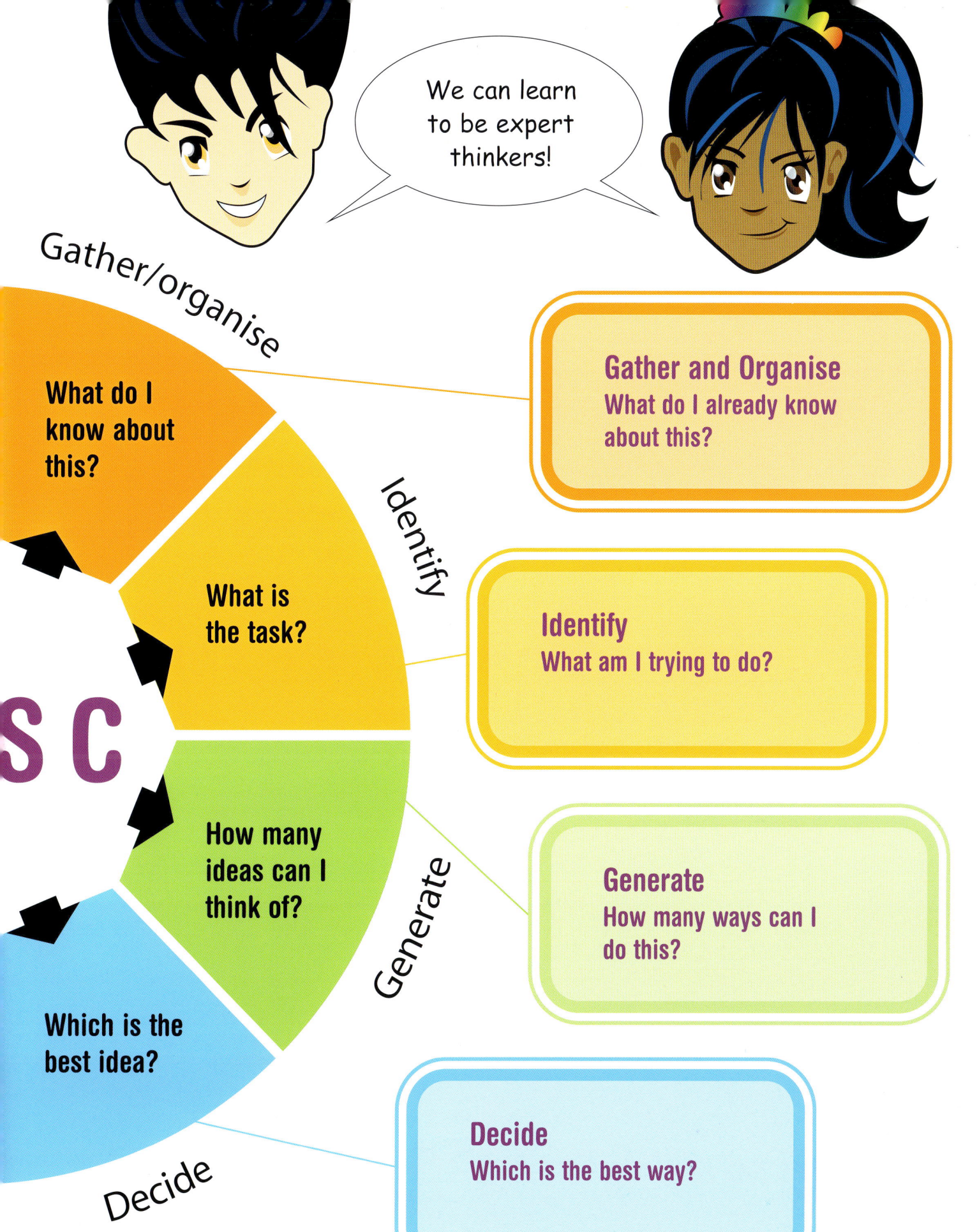

Gather/organise
What do I know about this?

Identify
What is the task?

Generate
How many ideas can I think of?

Decide
Which is the best idea?

Gather and Organise
What do I already know about this?

Identify
What am I trying to do?

Generate
How many ways can I do this?

Decide
Which is the best way?

TASC: Thinking Actively in a Social Context © Belle Wallace 2004

nace

What is NACE?

NACE is a charity which was set up in 1984. It is an organisation that supports the teaching of 'more-able' pupils and helps all children find out what they are good at and to do their best.

What does NACE do?

NACE helps teachers by giving them advice, books, materials and training. Many teachers, headteachers, parents and governors join NACE. Members of NACE can use a special website which gives them useful advice, ideas and materials to help children to learn.

NACE helps thousands of schools and teachers every year. It also helps teachers and children in other countries, such as America and China.

How will this book help me?

Brain Academy Supermaths books challenge and help you to become better at learning and a better mathematician by:

- Thinking of and testing different solutions to problems
- Making connections to what you already know
- Making mistakes and learning from them
- Working with your teacher, by yourself and with others
- Expecting you to get better and to go on to the next book
- Learning skills which you can use in other subjects and out of school

We hope that you enjoy the books!

Write to **RISING STARS** and let us know how the books helped you to learn and what you would like to see in the next books.

RISING STARS

Rising Stars UK Ltd, 22 Grafton Street, London W1S 4EX